GREECE

the people

Sierra Adare

A Bobbie Kalman Book

The Lands, Peoples, and Cultures Series

 Crabtree Publishing Company

The Lands, Peoples, and Cultures Series

Created by Bobbie Kalman

Editors
Virginia Mainprize
Ellen Rodger

Computer technology advisor
Robert MacGregor

Project development, writing, and design
Water Buffalo Books
Mark Sachner — editor
Sabine Beaupré — design
MaryLee Knowlton

Separations and film
Dot 'n Line Image Inc.

Printer
Worzalla Publishing Company

Ilustrations
George Balbar: pages 6-7, 8-9

Special thanks to
The Greek Tourism Office and Office of the
Minister of Business, New York; Gonda
Van Steen, Department of Classics,
University of Arizona; the Panos family;
Marsha Baddeley

Photographs
Susan Alworth: page 5 (all), 11 (bottom), 12, 14, 25 (top), 26 (bottom); Corbis-
Bettmann: pages 28–29; Marc Crabtree: pages 21 (top, bottom), 25 (bottom),
31; George Daniell/ Photo Researchers: cover; Farrell Grehan/Photo
Researchers: page 16 (top) Mike Jackson/Photo Researchers: page 11 (top);
Wolfgang Kaehler: pages 4 (right), 10, 15 (top), 17, 20, 23 (bottom), 27; Will &
Deni McIntrye/Photo Researchers: page 15 (bottom) Nimatallah/Art
Resource, NY: page 6: Photo Researchers: page 1 Carl Purcell: pages 4 (left),
13 (both), 16 (bottom), 19, 23 (top), 24, 26 (top), 30; Scala/Art Resource, NY:
pages 9 (), 7; Ingrid Mårn Wood: page 22.

Front cover: Donkeys are the best way of getting around the narrow streets
of many Greek villages.

Title page: Two men relax in the early afternoon at a local café on the island
of Santorini.

Back cover: Olives and olive oil have been part of the Greek diet since
ancient times. This vase, which was made in the sixth century BC, shows
men harvesting ripe olives by beating an olive tree with long poles.

Published by
Crabtree Publishing Company

350 Fifth Avenue	360 York Road, RR 4	73 Lime Walk
Suite 3308	Niagara-on-the-Lake	Headington
New York	Ontario, Canada	Oxford OX3 7AD
N.Y. 10118	L0S 1J0	United Kingdom

Cataloging in Publication Data
Adare, Sierra,
    Greece: the people/Sierra Adare.
        p. cm. -- (The lands, peoples, and cultures series)
Includes index.
Summary: Explains the daily lives of the Greek people, including
school, work, and family activities and covering everyday life both in
the city and the country.
ISBN 0-86505-307-3 (paper) -- ISBN 0-86505-227-1 (RLB)
       1. Greece -- Social life and customs -- Juvenile literature.
[1. Greece--Social life and customs.] I Title. II Series: Kalman, Bobbie.
1947- Lands, peoples, and cultures series.
DF78.A33 1999
949.5--dc21   LC 98-40369
                             CIP

Contents

The many faces of Greece

Over thousands of years, many **ethnic** groups from Europe, Africa, and the East have settled in Greece. Some of these people moved on to other regions, and some were conquered by more powerful **civilizations**. Many, however, stayed and mixed with each other over the centuries.

What is an ethnic Greek?

Today, ninety-eight percent of the people living in Greece are ethnic Greeks. They are descended from the ancient Greeks and the many non-Greek peoples who have invaded or lived in the area since ancient times. These groups of people have included the Persians, Macedonians, Romans, and Turks. This blending has produced the people known today as Greeks. They share a common language and practice the Greek Orthodox religion. These factors make Greece one of the most **homogeneous** nations in Europe.

Greeks abroad

Greeks are travelers and have settled in many countries. For centuries, there have been thriving Greek communities in Istanbul, Turkey, and Alexandria, the commercial capital of Egypt. Greek **immigrants** to Canada and the United States have brought their rich culture and traditions to their new homes. Wherever they are, however, Greeks cherish the memory of their homeland and dream of returning one day, even if only for a visit.

About ten million people live in Greece today.

Turkish Greeks

About five percent of Greeks are of non-Greek origin. They come from several ethnic and religious backgrounds. The largest of these groups, about one hundred thousand, is of Turkish descent. Turkish-Greeks are citizens of Greece. They speak the Turkish language and follow the teachings of Islam, the Muslim religion. Many Turkish-Greek women wear long black overcoats and white scarves, called *yashmaks*, that cover their head and shoulders.

Some of these Turkish Greeks live in Thrace, the province that borders Turkey in northeastern Greece. Others live on the Dodecanese Islands, which lie just off the Turkish coast. These islands were part of Turkey until 1947.

More than 60 percent of Greeks live in the cities. About four million people live in or around Athens, the capital city.

Jewish heritage

Greece has a Jewish community that dates back over two thousand years. In the late 1400s, many Jews left Spain because they were being **persecuted** for their religious beliefs. They settled in Greece, where they were allowed to practice their religion freely. The Jewish population of Greece grew to about seventy thousand. In the 1940s, the German invasion of Greece took a horrible toll on the Jewish population. The Nazis sent thousands of Jews to concentration camps, where they were murdered. The once thriving Jewish community was reduced to five thousand people.

Gypsies

Small groups of Roma, also called gypsies, are found in some parts of Greece. Gypsies speak an ancient language, called Romany. Many continue their nomadic tradition of traveling around the country with their animals and caravans. Others have settled in towns in the provinces of Thrace, Macedonia, and Thessaly.

Inside an ancient temple

The people of Athens built the Parthenon between 447 and 432 BC. It was a temple dedicated to Athena Parthenos, Athena the Maiden, the patron goddess of their city. The temple was and is a marvel of marble. Even the roof was made of marble tiles about an inch (2.5 cm) thick. Statues **adorned** the Parthenon both inside and out. In the *naos*, the inner room, stood a 40 foot (12 meter) gold and ivory statue of Athena holding her shield. To this day, the Parthenon sits on top of the Acropolis, the once-fortified hilltop in the center of Athens.

This is a copy of the statue of Athena. The original disappeared long ago.

Everyday life in ancient Greece

Centuries ago, daily life in the ancient Greek city-states was somewhat different from everyday life in modern Greece. However, there are some similarities.

The agora: marketplace and more

The *agora*, or marketplace, was the center of everyday life. It was a large open space in the middle of the town, surrounded by public buildings, offices, and shops. Early each morning, the agora began to fill with people. Merchants opened their shops, and villagers set up stalls, selling vegetables, wine, cheese, and live sheep and goats. Men on their way to work stopped for a chat with friends. By mid-day, the agora was a noisy, busy place. Shopkeepers called out their wares, trying to attract customers. Traveling acrobats and musicians entertained groups of curious bystanders. Men came to do the daily shopping, often with the help of a slave, who carried the groceries home. Because few homes had their own well, women came to collect water at the public well in the agora. Later in the day, people came to see a play at the open-air theater, work out at the gymnasium, or worship at one of the temples.

The agora was an ancient shopping mall or plaza! People shopped, attended public events, and visited friends in the agora. The roofed buildings with columns are known as **colonnades.** *Women met at the communal well to fill the family's water jugs.*

A work day in ancient Athens

Whether a man owned his own shop or worked for someone else, he woke up at dawn. After meeting his friends in the agora, he headed off to work. Men in Athens had many jobs. Some worked in government , some were potters who made and sold clay pots and urns and some made jewelry or shoes. Others were blacksmiths who made plows and weapons. The ancient Greeks preferred to run their own businesses and be their own boss. Some men, however, hired themselves out as day laborers. They worked on farms and in the vineyards.

The ground floor of this ancient Greek house contained a storage room, a courtyard, and a shop. The rooms on the upper floors were used for sleeping, weaving, cooking, and housing the family's slaves. The house opened up in the back into a large courtyard. The front of the house, where the shop is located, faced the crowded street.

Strong women of Sparta

In contrast to women in other city-states, women and girls in Sparta had more freedom. Because Sparta was a warrior society where every free man was a soldier, military discipline and physical training were very important. Women were encouraged to exercise so they could give birth to strong boys. At times in Sparta's history, women were allowed to meet with men outside their home and could even own property. Like all other women in ancient Greece, however, they were not allowed to vote.

Sweating and bathing

The ancient Greeks believed in the importance of a healthy body. At the end of the workday, men stopped off at the gymnasium for a work-out and a bath. At sunset, they returned home for dinner. Men ate separately from women and often entertained other men in the evening. In wealthy households, slaves served the food, and musicians and dancing girls entertained the guests.

Women stay at home

Ancient Greek women had few rights. They could not vote in elections and were expected to obey their husbands. They spent most of their

lyre, a small instrument that looks and sounds like the harp.

Boys stayed in school until they were fifteen. At eighteen, they became citizens of Athens and joined the army for one or two years. They could then take up a trade, work for the government, or if they came from a wealthy family, enter a sports academy.

Girls did not go to school. They stayed home with their mothers, who taught them to spin, weave, and cook. When they were about fifteen, girls married men who were usually twice their age. Fathers chose their daughter's husband, and the bride did not meet the groom until her wedding day.

At a time when women were taught only the basics of reading and writing, Sappho was an exception. She ran a school for girls on the island of Lesbos where they were taught music, singing, poetry, and writing. Sappho wrote nine books of poetry, and the Greek philosopher Plato considered her one of the greatest poets of the ancient world.

time at home, managing their slaves, if they were wealthy, or doing the housework themselves. Like many women today, they prepared the food, cleaned the house, and looked after the children.

Boys and girls

When they were six, boys in the ancient city-state of Athens were sent to school, where they learned to read and write. Instead of using a pencil and paper, they wrote on wax tablets with a stylus, a tool with a sharp end to cut into the wax and a soft end to rub out mistakes. With the help of an abacus, a calculator with counter beads that slide along rods, students studied arithmetic. Boys also took music lessons, learning to play the

Family life is very important to the people of Greece. Greek families maintain many traditions, especially in the villages. Mothers have a special position of honor. People tend to live close to their extended family, their grandparents, aunts, uncles, and cousins. Relatives give help and advice to each other. Older people are respected and often live with and are cared for by their children and grandchildren.

Wives and mothers

Some Greeks still consider women inferior to men. Women are expected to have children, especially sons who will pass along the family name to the next **generation**. Even today, when many women work outside of the home, they are responsible for taking care of the household.

Parents and children

Although parents are very loving towards their children, they raise them quite strictly. Until they are old enough to leave home, children, especially girls, are controlled by their parents. Fathers have the final word in making decisions. In their spare time, children are expected to help on the farm or in the family business.

The dowry tradition

Until recently, families chose their children's marriage partners. Today, most young people decide whom they want to marry but other marriage traditions continue. One of these traditions is providing a dowry. A dowry is money or property a woman brings to her husband when she gets married. Today, Greek

In most modern Greek families, fathers spend more time with their children than in the past. These kids and their father are feeding ducks at the National Garden in Athens.

Family and friends enjoy a meal together at a seaside restaurant in the Cyclades islands.

law limits the size of the dowry, forbidding any that will **impoverish** the bride's family. It is still the custom in southern Greece and on the islands, however, for families to give their daughter a house and furniture when she gets married. Some parents may give her their house and move to a smaller house or apartment. Others may rent an apartment in the same building or add a story onto their house for the young couple. Instead of a traditional dowry, some girls are sent to university in Greece or another country.

Too close for comfort?

In northern regions, the groom often brings his bride to live with his family. Moving in with her husband's parents can be a difficult adjustment for a young woman. Especially until she has children of her own, she may find she is bossed around by her *petherá,* or mother-in-law.

In some families, three generations live together. This tradition allows both parents to work outside the home while the grandparents look after the children.

Women in society

Except in Sparta, women in the city-states of ancient Greece stayed at home. They rarely appeared in public except at festivals and funerals. Usually with the help of slaves, women looked after the household chores, such as preparing meals, cleaning, and caring for the children. Women did not eat with their husbands. They lived in a separate area of the house which was not so well decorated as the men's section.

Not so different today?

Many Greek women are still tied to the home. They feel a great deal of pressure to marry before their late twenties and have children, especially sons. Even if she has a job, a married woman is responsible for cooking and cleaning, shopping, doing the laundry, and looking after the children. She shows her worth by keeping a spotless house. In some families, especially in the villages, fathers, sons, and male guests eat separately from the women. Greek cafés are often filled with men, drinking coffee or sipping *ouzo*, a strong alcoholic drink. The women are at home preparing dinner or finishing the housework.

The changing role of women

In the early 1980s, the **feminist movement** began to affect Greek society. Today, many women have jobs outside the home, but men, on the whole, are better paid. Most women work in low-paying jobs, such as clerks, secretaries, and factory workers. Some, however, are entering those professions that until recently were controlled by men.

In the cities and villages, many women run family-owned shops and restaurants.

Nannies for working families

Today, many Greek women work outside of the home, and fewer couples move in with their parents. Some young families hire **nannies** to live in the home and help care for the children. Especially in the cities, many parents want their children to have a **foreign** nanny. English- and German-speaking women are in great demand because they can teach the children the language and customs of another culture.

(above) Women from different generations examine the goods at a shoe store in Athens.

(below) Women are in the work force in ever-larger numbers in Greece today.

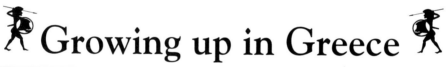 Growing up in Greece

Greek families, especially in the cities, are smaller today than they were in the past. Parents usually have only two children. Since many families live in the same village, house, or apartment building, relatives stay in constant contact with each other. Cousins play together and are as close as brothers and sisters. Children also grow up as part of a *paréa*, a group of tightly knit friends who usually go through life together. When a young woman marries, she may bring her new husband into her paréa and join his paréa as well.

Nameday parties

Greek children celebrate both their birthday and their nameday. In the Greek Orthodox community, every day is dedicated to a saint. On May 21, St. Helen's Day, for example, every girl named Helen celebrates her nameday. Her parents throw a party with food and sweets. Family and friends stop by with their good wishes, a card, or a gift.

What's in a name?

According to tradition, Greek parents name their first son after his grandfather on his father's side. On mainland Greece, the first daughter gets her father's mother's name. In the Aegean Islands, the first girl is traditionally named after her grandmother on her mother's side. Today, this custom may apply to one of the girl's middle names only, while her first name comes from a popular soap opera or television show! In the Greek Orthodox tradition, girls have one first name and two middle names.

Just for fun

In Greece, children do many of the same things for fun that kids do in other parts of the world. Kids play ball in the town square, skateboard in the streets, or play computer games with their friends. When the weather is nice, families go to visit relatives in the country or on another island. Parents or grandparents take the kids to the movies, the theater, or maybe the museum. They go out for ice cream, too.

(opposite page) **In some Greek communities, children grow up and go through life together as a paréa, a tightly knit group of friends.**

(right) **A woman relaxing with her children at home on an island in the Aegean Sea.**

(below) **A father and son out for a walk pass by posters on a street in Athens.**

(above) A stone house sits in a beautiful mountain setting.

(below) Homes on Mykonos come right up to and sometimes hang over the water that surrounds this island.

 # Greek homes

Greece is a land of contrasts: crowded cities and small farms, isolated island villages and sprawling mainland suburbs. The types of houses Greeks live in depend on the land, the climate, and the economic and cultural background of the people who own them.

Village houses

In villages, farmhouses are usually clustered closely together and are surrounded by fields and farmland. The flat-roofed houses are small, with three or four rooms, wood or earth floors, and a small kitchen. Many of these houses are simply furnished, with a few wooden chairs, a table, and low beds. The walls, floor, and furniture may be decorated with hand-embroidered fabrics and woven rugs.

In warmer regions, part of the kitchen may be outside the house, and most of the cooking is done in the open air. Families spend a lot of time outdoors. A small garden, a porch or balcony, or a courtyard are favorite places to eat meals, chat with friends, or just relax after a busy day.

Island and mountain living

In the mountains of the north, many homes have two or three stories and pointed roofs to keep the snow from piling up. The first floor is often a cellar or workshop. The second floor provides warm winter quarters for the family.

House styles on the islands are quite different, and they change from region to region. On Crete, far off in the southern Mediterranean, where the temperature gets very hot in the summer, the houses are wide and low to **deflect** the sunlight. On the Cyclades Islands, gleaming villages of flat-roofed houses cling to the hillsides. Large **cisterns** collect rain water off the roof. The winding lanes between the houses are often too narrow for cars. Motorcycles and the occasional

The rooftop terrace on this house is perfectly suited to the warm, sunny climate of Santorini, one of the Cyclades Islands in the southern Aegean Sea.

Ancient break-ins

Houses in ancient Greece were built of mud bricks on a stone foundation. Since the bricks were not baked, they were soft and easy for burglars to break through. Houses were built around a courtyard. Rooms looked onto the courtyard and not out onto the noisy, smelly street. The family lived in the back of the house. The women's quarters were upstairs.

donkey, laden with supplies or firewood, are the only way of getting around the village.

City homes

In towns and cities, where there is a shortage of housing, most people are crowded into apartment blocks that stretch as far as the eye can see. In the suburbs of Athens and other cities, wealthier families may have their own home. Usually, it is a two story building of concrete and brick, painted white or bright colors. Because their homes are often small, Greeks meet their friends for a coffee or a meal at the local café or **taverna.**

School days

For centuries, the Greeks have valued education. During the four hundred years that Greece was ruled by the Turks, schools were seen as one of the most important ways of keeping Greek culture alive. When Greece became independent after the revolt against Turkish rule, elementary school for all children became the law. Greece was one of the first European countries to take this step.

Elementary and high school

Children start school when they are six. In state schools, education is free. Some children go to private schools, especially if their parents want them to learn foreign languages. After six years of grade school, children go to the gymnasium, or high school. These schools specialize in different subjects. Some focus on Greek history, language, culture, and literature. Others specialize in science, while some are vocational schools, teaching commercial or technical skills.

Universities

The universities of Athens and Thessalonika are the oldest and most important ones in the country. Students must write a university entrance examination, and competition to get into university is stiff. Many students travel abroad for university.

A typical school day

The school bus picks up children around 8 a.m. In places where there is no school bus, public buses run before and after classes so that children can catch one passing close to their school. Students are expected to study hard and respect their teachers. During a short break, which is more like a recess than lunch, children have a snack and play outside until classes begin again. Younger students get home by 2 p.m., while older ones stay in school until 3 or 3:30. Many parents worry that Greek public schools do not teach as many subjects as other European schools. Even

The Greek alphabet

Greek children learn to read and write using an alphabet that is different from the letters used in most of Europe and North America. This Greek alphabet is very like the one used by the ancient Greeks. When Greek children learn a foreign language, such as French, English or German, they not only have to learn new words, but also a completely new set of letters, known as the Roman alphabet. To show you how hard this is, here are a few Greek letters.

Roman letter	Greek letter	Can you figure out which word spells?	
a	α	alpha	δελτα
g	γ	gamma	φι
d	δ	delta	ομεγα
e	ε	omega	αλπηα
l	λ	pi	γαμμα
m	μ	phi	πι
t	τ		
ph or f	φ		
o	o		
p	π		

Answers

alpha αλπηα
gamma γαμμα
delta δελτα
omega ομεγα
pi πι
phi φι

though it is very expensive, families often send their children to private school after regular classes end for the day.

Having fun in school

School is not only a time for studying and books. Greek children enjoy sports such as basketball, volleyball, and soccer. Students put on plays and concerts for their schoolmates and parents. Making holiday decorations, especially painted Easter eggs, is a favorite arts activity. A trip to the museum, the children's theater, or the site of ancient ruins is almost as good as a holiday.

School break by the seashore! Summer holidays are a time for relaxing and having fun. Summer breaks are between one and two months long, and during the year, school is often closed for religious, one-day holidays.

English shows its Greek roots

"It's Greek to me" is an expression people use when they do not understand something. About one-sixth of the words in the English language, however, can be traced back to ancient Greek. Here are some words commonly used in English that come from the Greek language:

Alphabet comes from the Greek word *alphabetos*. *Alpha* and *beta* are the first two letters of the Greek alphabet. An *alphabet* is the letters of a written language.

Bicycle comes from the Greek *bi*, which means two, and *kyklos*, which means wheel.

Drama comes from the Greek word *dran*, which means to act or do. A *drama* is a play performed on a stage.

Hippopotamus comes from the Greek words *hippos*, which means horse, and *potamos*, which means river.

Metropolis comes from the Greek word *meter*, which means mother, and *polis*, which means city. A *metropolis* is a "mother city," or major city.

Museum comes from the Greek word *mouseion*. A mouseion was a temple dedicated to the nine Muses, the goddesses who inspired writers, musicians, and scientists in ancient Greece. A museum houses works of art and historical importance.

Theater comes to us from the Greek word *theatron*. *Thea* means sight, and *theorein* means to look at. A *theater* is the building where plays are performed and watched.

Telephone comes from the Greek word *tele*, which means far, and *phone*, which means sound.

At Work

Because during much of the year it so hot in the middle of the day, Greeks start work early. In the afternoon, they take a break and go home for a rest. It is considered impolite to call on someone during nap time.

Open for business

For most shops and businesses, the day begins at 8 a.m. and ends around 2 p.m.— on Monday, Wednesday, and Saturday, that is. On Tuesday, Thursday, and Friday, most businesses shut down at 1:30 and reopen at 5 p.m. They close for the day at about 8:30 p.m. Companies that do business with other countries have recently begun to keep a 9 a.m. to 5 p.m. work day.

Being boss

Most Greeks prefer to own and run their own business. Instead of going to big supermarkets, they buy their groceries from someone they know. Villages, towns, and even big cities have family-owned butcher shops, bakeries, and grocery stores. In every neighborhood, there are many small shops and *períptera*, tiny booths that sell all sorts of products, from magazines, candy and soft drinks, to wrist watches, stuffed toys, and sunglasses.

Family affair

In family-owned businesses, every member of the family chips in and helps. Parents and grandparents take turns looking after the shop. In cafés and restaurants, father may cook, and mother and children serve the customers. It is quite common to see children aged nine or ten waiting at table or clearing the plates. If children are too young to carry plates, they sweep the floor or wipe the tables. Everyone helps wash the dishes.

A street vendor in the middle of a busy market selling pasteries.

(above) A group of men take an afternoon break at a coffee bar.

(below) A sidewalk períptera offers a variety of snacks, soft drinks, and other products.

Coffee time!

Greeks love coffee, but it is unusual to see a coffeepot in an office. Greeks prefer to order out. Waiters or shopkeepers in white aprons carry trays of *ellinikó kafé*, a very strong coffee topped with frothy, steamed milk, through the streets to neighboring offices.

Greek cities are busy places, filled with people, noise, highrise buildings, and traffic. Office workers rush to their job, groups of children wait for school buses on the street corner, and traffic police try to keep cars moving. Everyone seems to be in a hurry.

Importing trends

Xenomania is a Greek word meaning the love of things that are foreign. Nowhere in Greece is that love more obvious than in the cities. Everyday life for many **urban** Greeks is filled with items from all over the world. People standing on street corners or riding on buses talk on cellular phones. The streets are crowded with foreign cars, and the shops are filled with **imported** goods of every kind. People wearing clothes designed in Paris or New York walk alongside "urban cowboys" decked out in jeans, leather vests, and cowboy hats. Many visitors to the cities from the islands or the countryside say they feel nervous asking for directions. They can no longer tell a Greek from a foreigner!

Even in Athens, Greece's biggest and busiest city, everyday life has its quiet moments. In the Pláka district, a homeowner fixes a light on his house.

A sea of concrete

Greek cities are growing so quickly that they can hardly keep up with the thousands of people moving into them each year. In some sections, block after block of six-story concrete apartment buildings are home to many families. Often, the residents are related to each other — aunts, uncles, cousins, and grandparents all living in the same building.

A typical day

Morning starts in a rush. The children are getting ready to meet the school bus and mom and dad are heading off for work. Greeks are not big breakfast eaters, and family members might have a piece of bread with butter and honey, warm milk, or yogurt. Children take a snack to school, perhaps *spanikopita*, a cheese and spinach pie or some olives and cheese, but this is not lunch. When they get home in the afternoon, grandmother has a big lunch waiting for them.

In the evening, the family gathers together. Mom helps the children with their homework, and later, everyone relaxes in front of the television. Greek children have dinner later than North Americans, around 8 p.m., and are put to bed before their parents eat around 10 p.m. On the weekends, the children get to stay up later, and sometimes the family goes out for a meal and a movie.

(top) A narrow city street is crowded with shops and apartments.

(right) A child feeds ducks in a quiet city park.

 In the country

Children growing up in the country have fewer of the latest gadgets, such as video games and CD players, than city children. On weekends and holidays, country children work in the fields with their parents and learn to take on grownup responsibilities. They spend their free time at the agora, the main square of the village, where families shop, enjoy an ice cream, or chat with their friends.

Life in a mountain village

In many mountain villages, homes are built so close together that they share walls. Houses cluster around a square with a church at the center. Smaller churches and shrines dot the surrounding fields and hills.

Gypsies: an independent life

During the harvest season, gypsies set up roadside tent camps on the plains. They hire themselves out as day laborers. Although the pay is low, gypsies earn just enough money to allow them to continue their nomadic, independent way of life. After work each evening, the **encampment** fills with the delicious smell of food cooking on an open fire. Music and dancing continue long into the night.

Many mountain villagers earn their living by shepherding livestock or tending small farms. Others cultivate orchards of chestnuts, walnuts, peaches, pears, cherries, apples, and olives. In the winter, families earn extra income by knitting sweaters or weaving rugs that are taken to the cities and sold to tourists.

Living on the plains

For centuries, people have farmed the flat plains, the most **fertile** lands of Greece. They are hot and humid in the summer but muddy and drenched in rain in the winter. Farming families live in villages where the houses, like those in the mountains, are next to each other. Farmers may own their land, rent it from wealthy landowners, or work on someone else's farm. Each morning, both men and women ride donkeys or tractors out to the fields. During the spring, summer, and fall, farmers are busy all day planting, fertilizing their fields, spraying plants with **pesticides**, and harvesting their crops. In the winter, life is easier. Men play cards or discuss politics for hours in village cafés. Women have time to visit their friends and practice embroidery skills that have been passed down from generation to generation.

(above) A mountain village café caters to both locals and tourists.

24

Market gossip

Saturday markets in the country towns give
people a chance to meet one another and catch
up on the latest local news. Farmers from the
countryside set up stalls and sell their goods.
Women shop for the freshest produce and haggle
for a bargain. Groups of men sip strong coffee in
the local cafés. Bearded Orthodox priests, in long
black **cassocks** and tall black hats, mingle with
widows dressed in black and teenagers in jeans
and T-shirts.

In some small towns and villages, such as the
mainland town of Xainthi, people close off the
main square to traffic on Saturday evenings for
nifpazaro, the bride's fair. This custom originally
gave young men a chance to exchange looks with
girls of marrying age. Today, it offers the whole
community an opportunity to get together.

*(top) An open-air market sells all sorts of fresh fruit
and vegetables.*

(bottom) An Orthodox priest hurries across a street.

25

Island living

Until recently, people living on the Greek islands were very isolated from the mainland. On some islands, the occasional boat bringing supplies and food was the only contact with the outside world. Many islanders were very poor, supporting their families by fishing and raising sheep and goats. Many people left, seeking a better life on the mainland or in other countries. Today, life has changed. Regular boat service and car ferries bring tourists all summer long.

Busy summers

During the hot summer months, Greeks from the mainland and tourists from other countries flock to the islands. They come to sunbathe on the sandy beaches, swim in the crystal clear sea, buy souvenirs, and enjoy the warm hospitality of their island hosts. During these months, the shops, hotels, taxis, cafés, and tavernas are very busy, and islanders work long hours. Most businesses are family owned, and parents expect their children to help.

Lonely in the winter

In the winter, when squalls hit, the islands practically shut down. During bad storms, the sea is so rough that boats bringing food and supplies may not sail for days, even weeks. Most islands do not have hospitals, and when the boats cannot sail, helicopters fly people out in an emergency. People can feel very isolated, although after the busy summer, they are happy for a rest.

(top) The island of Hydra is known for its steep cobblestone streets and craft shops, selling carpets, jewelry, and pottery.

(left) A group of fishermen repair their nets on Skiathos, one of the Sporades islands.

Looking away from the sea

The sea, which has traditionally provided a living for islanders, suffers from overfishing. Fish are now caught far out at sea. Much of the fish that is served in Greek restaurants is imported from other countries and is actually cheaper than locally caught, fresh fish.

Dynamite: a tribute to the dead

When the sea claims the life of a fisherman or sponge-diver from the island of Kalymnos, a stick of dynamite is hurled into the sea from the top of a cliff. The explosion announces the death and honors the tragic loss.

The harbor of Skopelos, in the Sporades islands, is a jumble of white houses and small churches against a green landscape.

Pastimes and Sports

For thousands of years, Greeks have believed in the importance of exercise and sport. The ancient Greeks built gymnasiums and stadiums where men and boys trained every day. Some ancient sporting events, such as track, gymnastics, and discus and javelin throwing, are still popular.

Really rough

Some sports played in ancient Greece, such as wrestling and boxing, were much rougher than today's versions. Contestants were often badly hurt in a game called *pankration*, which combined wrestling with boxing and kicking. Biting and eye poking were all part of the game. The fight lasted until one opponent showed that he had been defeated by raising a finger — if he still had the strength. Some players even died.

Modern Greek games and sports

Soccer, which the Greeks call football, is the most popular sport in Greece today. Professional soccer matches take place almost every Sunday afternoon during the season. Basketball's popularity is growing fast. A favorite pastime for fans, even in remote villages, is to gather at the local café and watch international basketball games on television.

In Athens, there are horse races every Monday, Wednesday, and Saturday. Water sports are very popular among Greeks. Windsurfing and water skiing are growing in popularity. Swimming in the warm, clear waters off one of Greece's many beaches is another favorite activity.

Toys and pastimes

If Greek children made a list of their favorite toys, games, and pastimes, it would not be all that different from a list of things that European and North American kids like. Greek children enjoy riding bikes with their friends, playing with dolls, watching T.V., or going to the latest movie. They play ball games, such as soccer, basketball, and volleyball. In all but the most remote regions, video and computer games are probably the most popular pastimes for Greek children today.

A group of Greek school children play soccer. Known throughout most of the world as football, soccer is a favorite among Greeks as both a player and a spectator sport.

Worry beads

Throughout Greece, people of all ages can often be seen fingering a string of beads made of wood, amber, or plastic. Greeks find that handling these beads, called *komboloi*, calms and relaxes them.

In the last fifty years, Greece has changed from a depressed, war torn country, to a prosperous, modern nation. As Greeks look ahead to the twenty-first century, they know they will have to deal with the problems and challenges rapid growth has brought.

Leaving the farm

Because so many Greeks have moved into the cities, problems have arisen for both **rural** and urban areas. In the country, fewer young people are left to work on farms or in small, family-run businesses. In the cities, especially Athens, services such as education, housing, and transportation need to be improved. The nation, as a whole, is still behind western Europe in computerized record keeping, waste disposal, and providing an adequate supply of drinking water. Communication services, such as the telephone system, e-mail, and the internet, need to be expanded. Modern goods, such as computers, CD players and VCRs are available, but salaries for many Greeks are still low, and many people cannot afford these luxuries.

Facing the challenge

Greece is trying to find ways to deal with these problems. Highways and railroads are being extended into remote areas to connect them to the rest of the country. Greeks are trying to find ways of creating a healthier environment. To decrease air pollution, a major problem in Athens, people are allowed to drive only on certain days of the week, depending on whether their cars have odd or even-numbered license plates.

Over thousands of years the Greeks have dealt with many military, political and social challenges. They will handle the challenges of the future just as well.

Because Athens is often choked with air pollution, some downtown streets are closed to traffic on certain days of the week.

 Glossary

adorn To decorate

cassocks An ankle-length robe worn by some priests

cistern A water tank

civilization A well-developed state

colonnades A row of columns usually supporting the base of a roof structure

deflect To cause something to turn aside or bounce off

encampment A camp, usually a large one put up for temporary living

ethnic Relating to a group of people's race or cultural background

feminist movement The women's movement that works for equality for women in the job market, wages, education, and politics

fertile Producing good crops

foreign Coming from another country

generation A group of people having a common ancestor

homogeneous The same or a similar kind

immigrant A person who settles in another country

import To bring goods into a country from another country

impoverish To make poor

nanny A person who looks after children in the home

persecute To treat in a way that causes suffering, especially because of religious beliefs

pesticides Chemicals used to kill insects

remote Faraway, distant

rural Belonging to the countryside

taverna A Greek restaurant

urban Belonging to a.city

Index

1 2 3 4 5 6 7 8 9 0 Printed in the USA 5 4 3 2 1 0 9 8